My journey to Self

Shweta Navani

Presentation by *BookLeaf Publishing*

Web: www.bookleafpub.com

E-mail: info@bookleafpub.com

ISBN: 9789357616867

First edition 2022

*I want to dedicate this book to you, reader.
I want you to know that you're not alone.
We are all on the same journey together,
just on different paths. Thank you from the
bottom of my heart.*

ACKNOWLEDGEMENT

I want to thank the universe for bringing me to this point in life. You taught me to be quiet and listen and that is the best gift of my life.

I want to thank all of those who have disappointed me and let me down including my ex. I have learned more from you because I know what not to do. You have shown me how I want to be in this world by showing me the exact opposite.

Finally, I would like to acknowledge with gratitude, the support and love of my family - my parents, Akshna and Surendra; and my sister, Chandni. I still remember when the four of us first came to Canada together. I remember staying up and eating those yummy, delicious but also gross beans from the can. I hold those memories close to my heart. Also, I want to thank Ro for listening to me ramble on and holding space for me. I hope you keep your promise that one day we are going to be two old ladies living in a retirement home living our best lives. I love you all so so much.

PREFACE

For years I felt like I was not good enough so I tried to fix other people's problems. I hoped that making others happy would fill the hole inside me that I tried to ignore for years. Then came a moment of betrayal so painful that it took my breath away. I realized that pain had always been my greatest teacher. Pain taught me that my value came from being and not doing. In solitude, I found everything that I needed was inside me. These words that I have written are my truth. They are the lessons that the universe has taught me over the past three years. I hope you enjoy it!

Just like me

Is there anyone out there who is like me?
Do you also hate when things start to change?
Do you fear they won't ever accept you?
Do you also feel lost, as if you don't belong?
Fighting to prove yourself
But inside you know you'll never be good
enough.
Trying to love yourself despite your flaws
Finally ready to wake up
And face the truth
Life is just a dream.

Fly free

Caged bird fighting to fly
Can't breathe under the weight of love
Don't know who I am
So I become a mirror for those around me.
Looking up at the stars
And I think 'why me'
Feeling like a stranger in a crowd
And to those that I love
When will I be set free?

Imperfectly perfect

Thoughts crash together like waves,
Running out of time
Feeling like I carried out a crime.
Can you help me
Find my train of thought?
Stuck in my bubble
I lost my way
And got into trouble.
'Create a path out'
I hear you say
'And light your way
Out of the tunnel.'

The price of love

True love doesn't ask
For compromises
For you to betray yourself
Nor to abandon
Your values and beliefs.
My pain tells me
I didn't love me
Enough to give me
What I deserve.
Here I am naked and alone
And yet brave enough to love me.

Face everything and rise

I have been forged from fire
I have stood on that cliff's edge
Fighting to breathe.
I have been stabbed in the back
Faced my fears
Been reborn through my tears
I have nothing left to prove
My worth is not decided by you
So now through storms
I will sing and dance
In the rain.

Dear little me

Feeling lost and confused,
You think no one cares .
You lost your voice.
Feeling unsafe,
So you stay quiet and small.
Hoping someone will come
And help you breathe
No one came to you then
But I'm here for you now
To tell you that you're safe
To take off
The good girl mask.
You can cry,
You can scream,
You can speak up,
If they don't listen
You can leave.

Whirlwind

Open my eyes to the storm
Thoughts brush and slip through me.
The clock ticks but I can't feel it
A voice whispers 'Remember'
But I can't hear.
The fire starts but I can't see
"What's wrong with you?
Why can't you just do it?"
I hear you scream.
My skin tightens,
My heart races,
Wishing I was anywhere but here
Will I ever want to be me?

Who am I?

Thoughts go in and out of your head
Until you feel like you're losing your mind.
Who am I?
What do I want from life?
And what does life want from me?
Words come to the tip of my tongue
But I swallow them back.
They will brush me off.
A smile on my face
Make sure the mask stays on
So no one sees
Calm on the surface
But madness underneath.

Internal GPS

If you ever feel lost
Always know that
Your heart knows the way back.
When you're feeling lost
You'll find who you are.
So let go and lean
Into the feeling
And you'll know
What truly matters to you.

I'm feeling fine

They ask me "are you ok?"
But they don't really want to know.
So I say 'I'm fine"
'F' is for Fed up
of never feeling good enough.
'I' is for Invisible
because no one sees the real me
'N' is for Nervous wreck
that my demons will take over me.
And 'E' is for emotional
Because I don't know
If I will ever feel complete.

Pedestal

I put you on a pedestal
As if you were better than me
But you are not who I thought you'd be.
I don't see the light shining inside me.
You hid behind a mask as I did
And I pretended that we were a story.
But that story came to an end
And you saw the real me.

Now here we are
Once again the strangers we used to be.
What can I do
But learn to always choose me.

Happily ever after

Born into a world
That says "to be happy
Find someone to be with."
"To be a good person
Listen to those around you
And never to yourself."
"Get as much as you can, they say
And the world will be at your fingertips."

In the silence a voice cried out
"What about me?"
And that brought me to my knees
"We are one so be kind to all" said my child self
"And let us live in harmony."

Drowning

A force pulls me under.
Breath leaves my body.
Fog comes over me
And blurs thoughts in
my mind.
Swimming against the current,
Climbing a tree with flippers,
Trying to see through my tears
Fighting a battle I can't win.
My hand reaches out for help.
A voice screams out for comfort
But all I hear is
"Pull yourself together."

The way I am

I keep my head down
Trying not to weep.
I just want you to
See me as I am.
Now my thoughts
Won't let me sleep.
I want to say "No, stop"
But if I do
Will you see me as weak?
I feel my throat closing in
And now I can't breathe.
Will you still love me,
If I choose to just be me?

Bully

I listen as they whisper and laugh at me
So I find my refuge in stories.
The locker door is closed over my hand.
"How could you do this to me?"
I want to scream at them
"You were supposed to protect me."
Instead, you used me as your punching bag
And made me bleed.
Your pain is not my responsibility.
I'll use this as a lesson
And create a new beginning
So no one ever has to feel like me.

Pain into beauty

My emptiness brought me to my knees
And I say "I beg you, please."
You offer me your hand
And your eyes say "Trust me."
I'm watching the world burning
And when I turn to you
Your smile gives me peace.
"Why is it so hard", I ask you.
"Uncertainty is a part of life, you say
"But I'll hold your hand in the dark
And help you turn your pain into beauty.

Memories

Children giggle and play around me
My throat squeezes in gratitude.
Stars twinkling above me
My chest rises in awe.
The sun rises to greet me
My eyes burn with excitement.
A flower growing through the cracks
I feel joy rushing through my veins.
I remember being carried on his shoulders
And being silly.
I miss the way we would laugh together.
I wish I could relive it again.
If only I could bottle these moments
And keep them as treasures
So they would last forever.

North Star

Listening to my heart as it tells me
"You don't need to do anything, just be."
If I don't know how to take care of me
If I don't believe in my value
Then how would you?
So from this place of silence
I finally realize that
No one is coming to save me.
I am my own savior
Now and forever more.